PLAY THE GAME OF LIFE
TO WIN

God Success Inward Motivation

J TRENT WILLIAMS

Printed in the United States of America

ISBN: 9798872507321

10 9 8 7 6 5 4 3 2 1

EMPIRE PUBLISHING
www.empirebookpublishing.com

DEDICATION

Dedicated to my sister Leslie Renate Williams-Knight (June 12, 1963 – October 25, 2023). Protector & Giver – Life well lived

Life's Therapy, Therapy for Life:

God's Success through Inward Motivation

What does it profit to gain the world . . .

Success! Play the Game (Life) to Win: Find your Inward Motivation

Live to win in the game of life

ACKNOWLEDGEMENTS

We never accomplish anything of significance by ourselves. There are several people I's like to thank, who have had a considerable influence on me and my development to be the man that I am. I thank my Lord and Savior Jesus Christ, to whom I owe everything, my very existence.

All my life, my parents, Charlie and Eleanor Williams showered me with love and believed in me. They instilled in me values that emphasized the importance of love, honor, and respect for myself and others. They impressed upon me the value of perseverance and the understanding that I could not expect to receive without giving in return. Their teachings empowered me to have faith in my own abilities and to believe that I can achieve my dreams. Mom and Dad, I love you.

I want to acknowledge my siblings: my eldest sister, Lisa, monitor, affectionately known as everybody's boss; my sister Renate, giver, the protector and guardian; my brother Terrance; our information source; my brother Travis; our Mr. Jack of all trades and my baby brother, Torrey; the comedian. Growing up, we shared countless adventures that shaped my adventurous spirit, and I owe a part of it to all of you. Thanks for the memories that I will cherish forever. I love you guys.

To my lifetime friends, who have been instrumental in boosting my competitive spirit and serving as a source of inspiration, I extend my heartfelt thanks. Among the influential figures in my life are my extended family members, including Patrick my double brother-in-law and sisters-in-law, as well as nieces and nephews who have left an indelible impact on me. I deeply admire and sincerely appreciate all of you.

To my children, Jaylen and Camryn, have given me the greatest privilege, responsibility, and joy of my life, being a parent. By observing the strengths and flaws I've demonstrated, they have shaped their own life journey. I want you to know how incredibly proud I am to be your father.

The last shall be first. My bride, my queen, my BFF and wife for almost 30-years, Pamela Williams, your support has been unwavering. At the age of 6-years old, I claimed you would one day be my girlfriend as you sat in the back of your first-grade classroom, where my mom presided as your first-grade teacher. We were friends before we were lovers. We started dating after graduating from high school and we have had highs and lows, breakups and makeups. Thank you for being there for me always! I love you still and always will!

Contents

I BELIEVE IN MIRACLES

In the small southwest Georgia town of Camilla, it was 1965. My mother held me in her arms at 6-months old. She noticed a problem with my breathing. She described it as shallow breaths or a laboring in my efforts to breathe. Naturally, as with any mother and her infant child, she was concerned. She took me to the doctor to determine what was wrong. The doctor's initial diagnosis was a problem in my lungs and probably pneumonia. Pneumonia, a very serious illness, is even more critical in an infant. I was treated by the doctors for pneumonia.

After several days, my condition took a turn for the worse. More comprehensive tests were conducted and additional x-rays were taken. The doctor entered the room, as my mother was nervously bracing herself for what he was about to say. The test revealed a more serious condition. "Your son has an enlarge heart", he told her. "Your child's heart is more than twice the size of that of a normal infant." The doctor's prognosis was grave. The doctor said that he was sorry and that he did not want to give her false hope. He continued and told my mother that I was not expected to live past a year. My mom was told that there was nothing they could do to treat my condition. He told her, if she wished, he could refer her to the Augusta Medical Center (AMC) in Augusta Georgia. At the age of her early twenties, my mother had already encountered stories and accounts of children with this condition who had sadly lost their lives. The doctor took the necessary steps and made a referral to the AMC. Overwhelmed by a mix of dread and a deep sense of despair, my mother embraced me tightly, her tears streaming down her face.

In the days leading up to the initial visit to the Augusta Medical Center, my mother began to desperately cry out to the Lord, asking him to heal me of this condition. Willing to offer her own life if God would spare me, she continued to pray. While praying the day before leaving for Augusta, she heard from God. She describes it as a distinctively audible voice saying, "your son is healed." Nevertheless, her prayers were unrelenting. Arriving at the AMC, the doctors examined me and run test to verify previous diagnoses. They compared their x-rays and lab results with those of the doctors in Camilla and Albany. The doctors were totally amazed to find that there was no indication of a heart defect according to their examination results. Although the doctors could not find any abnormalities, they were not totally convinced that I was healed. The doctors said these things do not just go away and hearts do not just shrink down to normal size after a few weeks. The doctors decided they wanted to continue to monitor me and scheduled visits for me to return for follow-up exams every few months. After a couple of years of these visits, there were no signs of any kind of heart problem. Still not convinced that everything was okay, the doctors extended the monitoring but adjusted it to once a year. A few years later, the appointments were adjusted to once every two years. Then finally, after I turned 13 years old, they determined that there was no reason for me to continue any more visits. The doctors revealed that this case was unusual and for the past 13 years they wanted to study and document how I was doing to use as a reference in potential future cases they may encounter. The most important revelation would be for the doctors to recognize that God's healing power was at work.

God's Continuing Grace and Mercy

I have always known to be thankful for God's grace, mercy, healing, and protection. Recently, I have acquired a renewed zest and reverence for the Lord's mercy and power. May 2023, I stepped from my house into my garage. Waving to my son as he was driving up in the rain, I was not watching my step. I missed the step; lunging forward to regain my balance, my left knee gave way. I went flying into the back of my wife's car shoulder, head and neck first. My neck snapped backwards, and I landed on the concrete floor of my garage. Unable to move anything but my head, I felt helpless. I remember looking at my arm, having no feeling in it and unable to move it. I wondered did my arm come off my body. It was then I realized I could not move any part of my body. I was paralyzed from my neck down. My son came in to the garage and I called to him saying Jay I need your help. I told him I could not move. I asked him to roll me on to my back. As I lay on my back staring at the ceiling of my garage, I cried, "Lord, help me."

What has happened to me? My son ran into the house to get my wife. She called the paramedics. As I lay on the floor of my garage, slowly feeling began to return, first to my arms, then to my hands, next to my legs and then my feet. I lay there a few more minutes, and I asked my son to help me to my feet. What seemed like an eternity was probably only a few minutes at the most. I stood up and walked into the house. When the paramedics arrived, I was moving around just fine. I had pin needle pain running down my neck, into both arms and into my hands. After a few minutes that went away. I did not allow the paramedics to take me to the emergency room. Instead, my wife drove me. At the hospital, they ran some test, with imaging, x-rays and Ct scans. They were all negative. Other than a little soreness and mild neck pain for a few days, I was fine. In fact, 4-days later I was back jogging and working out at the gym. God covered me. He spared me from a catastrophic injury and even death. "Let the goodness of the Lord be known."

The medical situation as an infant and the freak accident in 2023 happened for a reason. The Lord allows events to occur to bring about a change in our lives. At that moment, we did not readily understand it. But, in time, as everything comes together, we can see how God orchestrates the events in our lives. My illness as an infant strengthened my parents and introduced them to His healing power. My mother and father discussed their childhood. They explained how their parents took them to church every Sunday and taught them to respect their elders and be kind to everyone. They were made to go to school and get good grades and earn their high school diploma and encouraged them to go to college. Although my parents were educated, morally sound, respected people in the community, they felt a desire for more spiritually. The Lord wanted to develop something in them. Those events that occurred a few months after I was born were part of the process of shaping and building my parents' faith and their ministry. The accident in 2023 ushered me into a place mentally and spiritually of a deeper appreciation for the presence of God and taking nothing for granted. "God is good and his mercy endues forever."

ACCEPT THE CHALLENGE

I grew up attending a Methodist church and learned the Apostles' Creed, which teaches salvation through Jesus Christ. There is little relevance to denomination when it comes to faith. The important thing is to believe in Jesus Christ as Lord and savior. In 1975, while still members of the Methodist church, my parents attended an organization called the Full Gospel Fellowship Ministries. Even at the age of 10, I remember my parents coming home from one of the meetings and have a renewed since of excitement about God, church, and Jesus. Not that anything was wrong with the Methodist church; my parents just seemed to have a renewed passion for God, his word and understanding God's promises. This revival came with a desire to dig deeper into the same bible they had been reading for years and learn more about God. My parents were so excited about this resurgence of their faith that they wanted to share it with their friends at the Methodist church. However, the parishioners at the Methodist church were more concerned about tradition and were unreceptive to the renewal that my parents had experienced.

I was approximately 10 years old. It was around this time that I invited the Lord into my life. I would gather all the neighborhood children and have a church on the patio of my home. At such a young age, many people would have considered us pretending or playing church. However, as an adult now, looking back, I can honestly say we were not play-acting. Those experiences of the presence of God were very real. In fact, there were children that accepted Christ then, that are serving the Lord today as adults.

High School

I was educated in the public school system in Camilla, Georgia, and graduated from Mitchell Baker High School in 1983. During my school days, I enjoyed playing a variety of sports and even making the varsity basketball team, where I was the starting point guard in some games. I was well rounded educationally, socially, physically and spiritually.

College

After high school, I visited several colleges and decided upon Albany State University, Albany, Georgia. It was late in the summer in 1983 and ASU had already completed their summer freshman orientation session. With the fall classes fast approaching, there was no time to waste. In a short amount of time, I had to submit an application, get accepted and register to start fall classes. I took an entrance exam, of which I did not score well, that coupled with my SAT scores of only 800, required me to have to take remedial courses to be accepted. It goes without saying that I felt ashamed. I felt like I was better than that. During my time in high school, I performed exceptionally well academically. I consistently earned A's and B's in my grades, with a few occasional C's. In general, I was a student who consistently achieved A to B grades. Every year at my high school's sports banquet, I would be honored with the Principal Award. This award recognized the athlete with the highest grade point average in their team sport. The problem I encountered was consistently underperforming on standardized tests like the SAT. Feeling embarrassed about having to take remedial classes, I reached out to my dad and asked him to come and pick me up from the campus. I had come to the conclusion that college was not for me and I determined I would enlist in the military. My dad told me that if that was my decision, then fine, he said he would take me to the recruiter's office that day. However, he also explained to me that I should not make a decision to do something that I perhaps did not want to do, just to avoid a challenge or what I thought was an embarrassing situation. He said that I should not make a permanent decision over a temporary circumstance and told me to go back to my dorm room and sleep on it and call him in the morning. He told me that no matter what my decision was, he would support me. After praying and thinking about it overnight, I realized I should not allow pride to consume me and cause me to avoid a challenge in pursuit of something I wanted. I called my dad and told him that once again; I had changed my mind and decided to remain in school.

I stayed in college, and with that decision came a desire to prove my worth. I decided I would no longer look back at missed opportunities, shortcomings, and previous failures. This was a new beginning, a revival of the sort. I want to prove to myself of my worth. I was not out to prove anything to anyone else. That approach gives the power of approval or acceptance to others, who oftentimes have no interest in whether you succeed or fail. That gives too much power to disinterested people. Attempting to prove something to others will always leave you second guessing yourself and questioning your worth and ability. My desire was not to show to anyone else, but to affirm within myself who I am and who I could become. I was motivated. I became hungry to succeed. I dug deep down into my inter-most being to find that inward motivation. I developed a passion for needing to win. I wanted to win. I had to win. No matter what it took, I had to find a way to win.

The biggest key to being successful is motivation. I am an avid sports fan. In sports, the team and/or the players that have the most success are not always the ones that possess the most talent or skills. The players who are most motivated and put in the hardest work are the ones who are most successful. Countless times I have watched sports teams who had less talent win championships, beating teams who were more skilled. This happened because they were motivated and worked harder. They were hungry. Something inspired them to give them the drive to push them to a level that they would not have achieved otherwise. One of the greatest examples of this was the "Miracle on Ice." In one of the most dramatic upsets in Olympic history, the underdog U.S. hockey team, made up of college players, defeated the four-time defending gold-medal winning, professional Soviet team at the XIII Olympic Winter Games in Lake Placid, New York. The reason the U.S hockey team could pull off the victory is that they were motivated, inspired, driven to push themselves to extraordinary limits.

The source of the motivation is sometimes external. A coach or mentor can stir you up and give you that inspiration or that drive to push you to succeed. However, many times there is no one there to give you that impetus that drive that push needed to take you the next level to be successful against what seems to be insurmountable odds. In this case, you have to find an inward (self) motivation. There has to be a stirring from the inside, an arousing of your innermost being, creating a hunger, a desire and eagerness, a push that drives success. The bible says in Matthew 5:6, "Blessed are those who hunger and thirst for righteousness, for they will be filled." Righteousness is defined as virtue, justice, rectitude, and blamelessness. This is what I hungered for.

My first year in college went well. Academically, I found an inward motivation because of having to take the remedial courses. Rather than sulk over what I felt was being dealt a bad hand, I used it as fuel to drive me forward. I was determined to prove to myself that I not only could pass my classes, but that I could perform on a high level. I completed the remedial courses in the first quarter and moved into the regular 101 college-level courses in the second quarter of my freshman year. I completed my freshman year, making the dean's list each quarter. I closed out my freshman year with a GPA of 3.55 on a 4.0 scale. Having to take the remedial courses turned out not to be a setback but a setup to ignite an inward motivation. I was presented with this challenge, which ushered me into a higher level of academic success, an academic level I might not have pursued otherwise. I used this obstacle as fuel for the fire that burned in me. I fought through the awkwardness and discomfiture of having to take the corrective classes. This strengthened me. I had to set aside pride and press to achieve my goals. I did not realize it but the negative experience of having to deal with remedial college courses was necessary to mold me into the person I needed to become to overcome the life challenges that lie ahead for me. In other words, I was being groomed and shaped for success, to persevere. God allows us to go through things to guide us into our destiny. I realize that what seems to be a setback is more of a setup to win over the long haul. So, no matter what the circumstances or the situation looks like, don't quit, don't give in, but find that inward motivation, that drive and push yourself forward.

DON'T SETTLE

Seeking Work

During my sophomore year, I realized the financial strain my parents had to endure by supporting three children in college at the same time. So, I started looking for ways to help by earning some money. I investigated several opportunities. I enrolled in Army ROTC at the university. The Army ROTC would offer me the chance to earn money while in school to help with tuition, books, and other expenses. ROTC seemed like an excellent option. At graduation, I would be commissioned as a second lieutenant in the US Army. This would give me a job to start my career. This plan seemed reasonable and logical. I also went to the university job counselor's office and signed up to participate in the cooperative education program. I thought this would be a great opportunity to earn money for college and acquire valuable work experience in my field of study. These options were good. I also believe that any of them would work for me. However, my prayer was for God to open the door that was best for me. I did not want to simply pursue the good idea. I wanted to pursue God's ideal solution for me. So, being proactive, I begin working on all of these options. I understood that I not only needed to have faith that God could and would bless me with opportunities, but I had to put some plans in motion. I had to be proactive. I could not just sit back and wait for something to just fall in my lap. So, I got busy.

While enrolled in ROTC, I competed for various scholarships. There was one scholarship in particular, called the Guaranteed Scholarship. To earn this scholarship, I had to compete against other ROTC student both at my university and other universities across the state. I was one of 20 finalist selected for the guaranteed scholarship, four from my university and 16 from other colleges and universities. When all was said and done, I won the scholarship. I was so very proud of my accomplishment. I was held in high esteem by my fellow ROTC cadets and the university's ROTC faculty.

Shortly after winning the scholarship and prior to signing the contract, I got a call from the universities counselor's office. I was granted an interview for a job under the cooperative education program (coop). This was exciting. I was not given a choice of two great opportunities. This is just what I had been praying for. Now I had to decide which career path to take. This was a good problem to have. I followed through with the interviews for the coop job. As a result, I got a job at the local military base. At this point, I was excited to have to have gotten this job. Typically, the way the cooperative education program works is, you work full-time one quarter or semester and go to school full time the following quarter or semester. The student continues to alternate each between the two until graduation. This situation usually delays or prolongs the time to graduate. However, the delay is well worth it, considering the income earned while in college and the work experience you gain along the way. In my case, I am working as a cooperative student in the same city that I am enrolled in college. This means that I can continue to take classes in the evenings during the same semester that I am working full time. This would allow me to not have to fall behind in the time it will take me to graduate. "Perfect!"

EXPECT THE UNEXPECTED

I was offered the coop job. I had successful outcomes in both ventures. I was super excited. Things were working in my favor. Having to now choose between the scholarship and the coop job, I turned down the ROTC scholarship and took the Coop job. It would be an understatement to say that the ROTC faculty and staff were upset with me for turning down the guaranteed full scholarship offer. The Coop seemed like a better fit for what I wanted to do.

I started working at the military base in my new coop job, and after the first few weeks, things had gone very well. I had completed my initial training. Exercising the work ethics I had been taught, I arrive to work early and was prompt with completing my assigned tasks. At the end of my first month, I met with my supervisor and got a very positive and glowing review.

Later, arriving at work one morning, I got a phone call to report to the human resource department. I asked my supervisor if he knew what it was about and he said that he was told that there was a question about my eligibility to participate in the coop program. When I arrive at the HR department, the HR director informed me I will have to be terminated. The reason she gave was that they discovered an oversite. I was not eligible for the coop program because my father works on the military base. She further explained that because of a nepotism regulation that children of parents employed by the base are ineligible to participate in the program.

Bewildered, confused, and totally disappointed by this news, I contended that this cannot be happening to me. I explained that as I went through three stages of interviews; I spoke with each interviewer about the fact that my father works on base and none of the interviewers expressed a concern or indicated that there was a problem. I protested that this nepotism rule could not be the case. It certainly was not applied consistently, since within the very department that I worked, an entire family worked together. A father was a department supervisor, while the wife and daughter worked in the department directly under his supervision. The human resource director explained that there was a difference between employment under regular base hires and employment hired under the cooperative education program. She went on to say that the nepotism rule did not apply in regular base hire situations because they were not working under the cooperative education program. She told me that the nepotism employment disqualifier was only applicable in the coop program. That did not seem fair to me at all. The director informed me that there was nothing more that she could do except collect my base identification and terminate my credentials.

I left work that day dejected and frustrated, but determined to fight for what I perceived to be fairness. After I got home from work, I talked to my dad and explained to him what happened. He too was floored by the news. I told my dad that I planned to return to the base the next morning and request to speak with the base commander and get an explanation from the person in charge, "the top dog." My dad told me I had his full support in whatever I decided to do.

BUILDING CONFIDENCE
IS A PROCESS

The Next Morning

When I came back to the base the next morning, I was surprised to learn that the base commander, the lieutenant colonel, was out of town. The officer in charge of civilian personnel stated that the base commander will be absent for a duration of two weeks. The personnel officer acknowledged my persistence and re-issued my base clearance and credentials, instructing me to return to work temporarily while awaiting a decision from the base commander. I was informed that my employment reinstatement was temporary. They gave me the opportunity to work again until I could make an appeal to retain the job. Despite the temporary nature, I felt vindicated. I sensed a righting of a wrong. I returned to my desk, settled in, and got back to work.

As I was working, I questioned God. Why was such a simple and normal process of working in a cooperative education job turning into a complex matter? I knew of dozens of other students who had completed this process and had pursued lucrative endeavors, advancing their careers. I told God that I trust him. I not only trusted Him, I dug deep inside of myself and find the motivation to move forward. I found that inward motivation.

Shortly after returning to my desk, one of the area supervisors asked me to come to her office to talk. I walked into her office and she tells me how she was disappointed that the base was taking away my job. She encouraged me to stand up and contest their efforts to take away this career opportunity. She told me she wanted to give me more advice, but she was afraid that if others discovered she advised me, she could be reprimanded or even fired. She explained to me she had firsthand knowledge of how similar situations had unfolded in the past, much like mine, and mentioned she was aware of the fact that the others in charge were only granting me a temporary extension in my job. They were planning to permanently dismiss me once they got there "ducks in a row".

In order to protect herself, she stated she would arrange for someone else to contact me and offer guidance on how to confront those who were trying to snatch away this opportunity. I went back to my desk and resumed working. Some time passed, and then a man approached me and gave me a note instructing me to meet him by the water fountain in five minutes. That was quite odd. As I approached the water fountain, I noticed a man standing with his back towards me, gazing out of the window. He politely requested that I avoid making eye contact with him or initiating a direct conversation. The man explained that he was asked by the supervisor that spoke to me earlier to come over and give me some information. He informed me he planned to place an envelope on the water fountain, instructing me to retrieve it after he had left. This event had a secretive atmosphere reminiscent of "Mission Impossible" or a "James Bond" movie. However, I followed his instructions exactly. The instructions told me to compose letters to my US congressional representative and senator, detailing the situation I am experiencing at the base. I mailed the letters to the offices of both my representatives.

Meanwhile, I met with the base commander. He extended two options. The first option was for me to apply for a formal waiver of the nepotism rule based on it being an oversight by the base human resource department; including the fact that I had found my niche in my job at the base. The second option was for me to ask the base to allow me to work there on a coverup of the nepotism rule. I explain to the commander that I was a man of integrity and did not want to request anything that was not ethical. So, I asked him to allow me to pursue the waiver based on the oversight and me finding a vocation in the coop program.

As it turned out, I was not granted the waiver, and I was terminated from the job. A few weeks later, I got a response from both my senator and my congressional representative. They both said they were very sorry that I had encountered the difficulties I was going through. However, there was not much they were going to do to impact my situation. I pondered to myself, that was completely pointless, just a draining and futile endeavor, utterly useless. Upon further reflection, I came to understand that it had value. To be honest, the experience taught me a great deal. I've discovered that we frequently encounter situations that are just a natural part of our growth and development. You see, with God's help, I was able to muster up the courage to meet with the base commander and reach out to both my senator and congressional representative. It was part of God's plan for me to grow and develop in those areas, ultimately shaping me into a strong and assertive individual who will benefit me in the future.

Indeed, I was learning an important life lesson. All of our efforts won't always bring the results that we expect or view as being successful in our own minds. We may perceive them as wasted efforts or failures. Yet, these situations play a vital role in our development, getting us ready for what lies ahead. It's crucial that we stay determined and not let frustration make us quit or settle. His plan was to develop me for the future. Hence, it can be inferred that the endeavor was not futile or lacking in significance. The experience was not only meaningful but also highly beneficial for my personal growth and development.

FROM A GOOD PLAN TO GOD'S BETTER PLAN

God will allow doors to be closed in order to lead me into a better situation. God worked things out on my behalf, even when I didn't see it. I continued to work with the office of career development at the university to find a job and work experience to go along with my degree upon graduation. So, I checked in with them weekly to see if any opportunities came across their office.

There were lots of people placed in my path who were instrumental in my development. One was the university's Dean of the College of Business. We developed a friendship that continued even after I graduated. Besides being the Dean of the university's college of business, he was also the pastor of a Baptist church. The Dean, a white southern Baptist pastor, invited me to attend his church in rural South Georgia. I only mention his race because it applies to what has often been regarded as the racially divided southern part of our country, more so that other parts of the United States. I accepted his invitation and attended one of the services. The parishioners were nice and cordial. They seem to work hard to show me that I was welcome. The order of service was traditional Southern Baptist. It was no different from the other Baptist services I had attended at the black Baptist church. He invited me to come back and visit again in the future.

THERE'S SUCCESS IN HUMILITY

JC Penney Company

As a student in the College of Business, I would stop by and talk to the Dean from time to time. I talked to him about my courses and other scholastic activities. All of which he seemed to take an interest in. So, I let him know I wanted to find an internship to get work experience in my field of study. I told him I preferred a paid internship because I could certainly use the money to help with my expenses. I requested his advice and direction as to how I should pursue or seek opportunities to get work experience. He told me about a fortune five hundred retail department store that had a management intern training program. He suggested that I just ask if they had any openings, as he did not know if they had any current openings, but it would be worth a try. So I put on a shirt and tie and a pair of dress slacks and went to the department store. When I got to the store, I asked one of the sales associates for the name of the store manager. After getting the store manager's name, I went upstairs and spoke to the receptionist. Referring to her by name, I asked if I could speak to the store manager. The receptionist asked if I had an appointment. I told her I did not have an appointment. After explaining that I could not see the manager without an appointment, she inquired about the purpose of my visit and assured me she would pass along a message. I inquired with the receptionist if it would be possible for me to make an appointment and return at a later time. The receptionist said she could take my name and number and call me later. It was at that time that I heard someone from the back office say, "Who's there that wants to speak with me?" A lady, dressed in a business suit and wearing heels, came down the hall. She introduced herself to me as the store manager. She said, "Young man, what can I help you with?" I told her my name and explained that I am a college student and I am looking for work. I told her I was very interested in an internship if she had such a position available. She explained to me she previously had an internship position opened; however, she had just filled the position a month earlier.

At that point, I felt I had just missed out on yet another opportunity. I thanked her for her time and asked her to consider me if she had any opportunities to come in the future. Feeling a little dejected, I started to exit the store, and as I made my way downstairs, just before leaving the building, the receptionist called for me over the store intercom. She asked me to return to the upstairs reception area. When I got back upstairs, the store manager asked me if I would be interested in being a part-time worker as a stock worker/janitor. She explained, the job required me to bring merchandise to the sales floor from the stockroom, as well as wash the windows and clean the bathrooms daily. I told her I would be very interested in that job. She said come back the next day in jeans and tennis shoes and she would put me to work.

YOU CAN GET THERE
FROM HERE

Although this was not exactly what I had in mind, I felt that if I could get my foot in the door by working there in some capacity, then maybe, just maybe, it could open up other opportunities for me later. I dug deep to find motivation to accept what may have been considered less to create a bigger and better opportunity later. I came to the realization that sometimes it is more advantageous to embrace what one might perceive as lower positions or minor roles, and gradually advance from there. By taking this route, you will learn humility and develop a deeper appreciation for future appointments. I dedicated a considerable amount of effort to demonstrate a strong work ethic, which involved consistently arriving on time and diligently fulfilling all of my responsibilities.

Six months later, the store manager called me to her office and told me she had observed my work over the last six months. She made note of the fact that I had a strong track record of timeliness and excellence in the completion of my assigned tasks. My work ethic left such a strong impression on her that she went ahead and requested a second intern position from the district office, and to her delight, they granted her request. In her conversation with me, she mentioned that she would be transferring me to the Young Men department, specifically as a management intern. By participating in this internship, I would gain the necessary skills and knowledge to excel in the role of merchandise manager. In addition to receiving a raise, I was fortunate enough to secure full-time hours, working a total of 40 hours per week. Furthermore, I was granted the flexibility to adjust my work schedule to accommodate my classes at school. The school/work setup I have could not have been any better, and I am extremely grateful for it. Despite God closing the doors on the good job with the cooperative education program, He opened another door for a better job with the internship. If I had not been terminated from the coop job, my decision to pursue this internship would have been completely different. It is significant to acknowledge that this was not a quick happening. I had to work as a stockman/janitor for a period of 6 months before finally being granted the opportunity to participate in the management internship program. While I was working as a part time stockman/janitor I was not sure when or if I would ever be given an opportunity to get an internship. The store manager had not made any commitments or assurances to me. Maintaining faith becomes even more crucial when it feels like everything is working against you. Even in moments when you may not be able to recognize it, it is crucial to understand that God is constantly orchestrating things in your favor. God, through His miraculous intervention, resolved a situation for me that, on many occasions, had seemed utterly impossible.

I was reminded of the story of King David. He started his journey as a shepherd before eventually becoming the crowned king. He was chosen by God. Even though he had been chosen as the future king, he was still required to go back into the field and tend sheep for quite a while. His promotion was not a sudden occurrence, in other words, it did not happen overnight. Despite the challenges, he stayed motivated, humble, and determined. So, when the time came, he was ready to lead and accept the responsibility that he was given. I accepted this as my time in the field and that

I was being prepared and groomed for what was in store for me. I was motivated!

I accepted the part time position, which allowed me to be noticed by the store manager, which led to me being offered the internship. I think God rewarded my humility. I was willing to accept a job much less than the one I was initially seeking. Working the part-time job, cleaning bathrooms, washing windows gave me a lesson in humility. Proverbs 22:4 says by humility and the fear of the Lord is riches, and honor and life. I worked the part-time job and did the work as unto the Lord. I worked that job to the very best of my ability and did not treat it as "just a part-time job." As a result, God elevated me to the level I desired. Sometimes God allows us to go through situations for us to show where our heart is towards glorifying him. God closed the doors to the coop program because he had a better plan for me. A plan that was a better fit for what I desired. God knew my heart's desire and delivered it. I worked as a full-time intern for the next three years until I graduated. It was difficult, but I was able to graduate with honors. Psalm 37:4 says: Take delight in the Lord, and he will give you the desires of your heart. I did indeed graduate as a Cum laude honor graduate. Remember, four years earlier, I had almost decided not to attend college. I had intended to take a different approach to bypass the challenge and what I perceived as an embarrassing requirement of taking remedial classes to begin my college journey. Rather than giving up or quitting, I found motivation. I searched within and discovered my inner motivation that drove me to succeed. Once again, it was difficult, but nothing truly rewarding comes easily. What mattered was my determination to not give up or quit. Remember, whatever you do, don't give up, don't quit, believe in you, have faith, complete what you start and finish strong.

TAKING THE WORLD BY STORM

After graduation, I thought I was ready to take the world by storm. After all, I am an honor graduate with a Bachelor's of Science Degree. Not to mention, having three years of management experience with a major Fortune 500 company, who by the way, promised to offer me a full-time job after graduation, once successfully completing the training program. Everything was established perfectly, wasn't it? What could go wrong?

Well, things do not always go as smoothly as you expect. The process should have gone like this. If there was not a permanent position open for me at the store I was working, the store's general manager, who was the director of the intern training program, would establish opportunities for interviews through the company for a permanent position elsewhere. That did not happen. I am not sure if he was just too busy or uninterested in my progress. I think it was the former. Although my advancement was his responsibility, he was under so much pressure to keep the store performing at a high level; I am sure my job placement became secondary on his list of responsibilities. Under the circumstances, I did not condemn him. So, I sought for a job placement for myself and reflected on the things I went through years earlier. I thought about how I had to fight for the opportunity with the coop job. I thought about how I had to request a meeting with the base commander. I thought about how I wrote letters to my United States congressional representative and senator. I could see how those events had helped to prepare me for this situation. Those events, as I was going through them, seemed fruitless, worthless, a waste of time. However, now, as I reflected on them, I see how instrumental those events were in preparing me for a time such as this. Those experiences that seemed to be failures taught me courage, boldness, and gave me confidence and self-assurance. So, it's important to know that when you go through difficulties and even fail to reach your intended goal, don't be discouraged. You are being developed. You are going through a procedure. Trust the process of God's plan for you. I felt I was left alone with no support. I had to fend for myself, but I was motivated.

I searched around the district and the region, within the company, for job openings and set up interviews for myself. After several unsuccessful interviews and months of failed attempts to get a permanent job, I'll have to admit I was frustrated. However, I did not quit, give in, or settle for something less than what I desired. I continued to seek a job with my current company, which was in retail management. During my search, I remembered that while I was in college; I had an interest in a career in banking. While I was in college, I did a case study that involved a story about a banker. The things I learned about banking intrigued me. Personally, I considered the prospect of a career in banking to be an incredibly interesting and compelling choice. In my job search, I took the initiative to apply for and interview at multiple financial institutions. After a duration of about nine months, I was pleasantly surprised to find myself in a situation where I not only received one job offer, but I received two job offers almost simultaneously. That's right, my current employer, finally offered me a job in the retail field and I also got a job offer with another fortune five hundred company, in the area of finance. While it may not have been a bank, it was indeed a job in the finance field. Let me tell you, my excitement was beyond measure. It was in that instance when I had an epiphany and understood that the time it took to receive a job offer from my current employer after the internship was not a setback, but rather an opportunity for personal growth. The timing of the job offer in retail being delayed was a divine arrangement, as it allowed me the opportunity to receive an offer in the finance field, which aligned more closely with my personal aspirations. Even though I persisted in my efforts and didn't give up, I could not help but feel frustrated when JC Penney didn't give me a job offer earlier. You see, had I received the job offer in retail earlier, I would have never looked for a job in the area of finance. God, in His divine wisdom, was orchestrating the events in my life to bring about positive outcomes for me, even when they were not apparent to me.

I wanted to pursue a career in finance, so I accepted the job.

THERE ARE VARIOUS ROADS TO SUCCESS SO DON'T BE AFRAID OF CHANGE

I begin my training with my new employer and my first job was an account service representative in the collections department. I was the bill collector for automobile loans. All of my collections were done by phone. That was a tough job. I was assigned thousands of accounts for people who had financed automobiles. My job was to make sure that the accounts that were assigned to me paid on time and were current each month. The company assigned me with the task of making every effort to bring the account current by collecting the payment from the client. The goal was to not have any account more than 30-days past due. When an account reached 90-days past due, it was critical and had to be assigned for repossession. My mild-mannered personality made this job tough for me. I had to demand payments from clients who didn't have the money for whatever reason. Some clients had extenuating circumstances that cause them to not have the money to pay, such as loss of a job or unexpected medical expenses that caused them to fall behind in their automobile payments. There were others who just did not pay because they did not prioritize making their payments on time. In order to keep my job, I had to make sure that at the end of each month, my delinquency rate was below a certain percentage. I had to bring the accounts current by whatever means necessary. Bring the accounts current meant offering payment extensions, due date changes and, when the account became critical, repossession.

The first month or two, I didn't do so well. My mild-mannered personality made it difficult for me to be as firm as I needed to be successful as a collector. I have always been a very compassionate person. During my childhood, I often befriended those who didn't seem to have any friends or who seem to be less fortunate. So, being a firm and tough collector was very hard for me. However, I did not want to fail. So, got out of my comfort zone and dug deep within myself for some inward motivation and learned to be firm. I learned to be a firm but compassionate collector. I was motivated.

I want to be clear that this success was not instantaneous, and I do not want to create the false impression that it was. On the contrary, it took me several months to successfully make this adjustment. Despite the challenges, I persevered and eventually became one of the top collectors in the department. It is rather amusing to think about the ups and downs when I look back on everything. I have a distinct memory of a particular month during which I was facing many challenges in my quest to reduce the delinquency rate. Within my portfolio, I had repossessed a grand total of 62 cars. I remember my supervisor saying, "good Lord man, you can't repossess every delinquent account." I learned to successfully work with the delinquent clients to bring their accounts current, rather than repossessing the automobiles. This gave me a sense of reward and gratification.

From Good to Better

Although my job was very rewarding, in the back of my mind, I still had a desire to pursue a banking career. I wanted to change from my good job to a better job. So, I left work on my lunch break and attended a local job fair. I handed out my resume' and spoke briefly with several banks that were in attendance. A month or two later, one bank called and asked me to come in for an interview. I certainly was not expecting to receive a call. Naturally, I was excited to hear from the bank. So, I went in for the interview. Prior to going in for the interview, I researched this bank and learned that it had the most comprehensive and respected bank management training programs in the United States. I was impressed by the reviews I read about the bank's training program. The bank was a large regional bank, whose headquarters were in Atlanta, Georgia and had multiple branch offices in three states, Georgia, Florida and South Carolina. Over the next couple of weeks, there were 3 or 4 additional interviews with different managers and executives at the bank. The final interview was with the bank's president and the senior executive vice president.

"Albany is not ready to be a progressive community"

In the interviews, race was discussed. The bank's top executives wanted to know how I would handle working in a predominantly white banking field in South Georgia. Keep in mind, although this was in the late 80s, the race struggle was tough across the country, but especially in South Georgia, and still is today. I felt their questions were fair. During the interview, the senior executive vice president made a statement and then asked a question of me. He explained to me he had been in banking for over thirty years in this community, and that to his knowledge, I would be the first black person to be a commercial lender in this city of Albany, Georgia. He went on to say that many of the people in the black community, including the black leaders and elected officials, may look to me to be the savior or their financial renaissance. His question was how I would handle the pressure of being the person who the black community is expecting to deliver the financing they felt they had been neglected for years. He continued, "this will create a lot of pressure and the expectations will be great on both sides of the racial divide in this community."

All eyes will be on me, watching to see if I will fail or succeed. On both sides of the racial divide, some wanted and expected to see me succeed and some wanted and expected to see me fail. My answer to his question probably sounds politically correct, but it was how I honestly felt. During our conversation, I made it clear to him that my intention was to adhere to the bank's established guideline in order to ensure fair and sound decision-making, regardless of factors such as race, gender, or ethnicity. There would be a continued focus and attention on the subject of race. I was not bothered at all by the fact that we continued to discuss race; in fact, I was glad that it was being discussed. If race had not been brought up, it would have signaled to me that they were ignoring "the elephant in the room" race, and an issue that was very important to the job. I felt a great sense of encouragement when I realized that they were able to acknowledge the existence of the problem. I would have been disappointed if they had not acknowledged that race was an issue.

One of the first things the bank president said to me was that Albany was not a progressive community. Indeed, he vocalized it audibly for all to hear. In other words, he was affirming his opinion that Albany was a racist community. It goes without saying that this was not a surprise to me. I already knew that to be true. I was taken aback when he openly acknowledged it, and it was encouraging to hear him admit that the problem existed. The fact that they expressed

31

a desire for things to change was a source of encouragement for me. In his statement, he acknowledged the presence of a specific subset of individuals, including both black and white individuals, who are in favor of Albany embracing diversity and having a broad-minded approach. However, he also noted that the broader community does not share the same stance on racial diversity and equality. He inquired about my strategies for achieving success as a banker in a community where a significant number of individuals held such a mindset. How could I be successful knowing that I will need to gain the support and trust of the whole community and not just one group or segment?

I provided my answer, explaining that I have no ability to alter the color of my skin and even if I did, I would not have any inclination to do so. I expressed to him that I am very proud of my authentic self and feel completely comfortable in my own skin. I did not intend to prioritize anyone's perception of me or seek their validation or approval. My main objective is to earn respect from the company, the community, and the clients. The purpose of my role as a banker is to treat everyone fairly and create a level playing field for all. I expressed my understanding that I cannot rewrite history or make reparations for any past injustices. My goal was to leverage my knowledge to educate and empower anyone I encounter, enabling them to thrive in their banking and financial ventures. It is important to note that I understood the significant lack of funding available to minorities, especially in the business sector. Despite the many strides that have been made, there is still work to be done.

YOU HAVE TO BE IN TO WIN

I understood that if I wanted to be involved in making a difference; I had to be in the game. The gap I am referring to is the financial injection that clients require in order to qualify for or obtain the loans. You cannot just open the door and declare that everyone is eligible for financing as long as they have good credit and the required capital. Unless you provide support to those who have always been rejected and never had a chance to build any capital or assets. Until this gap is bridged, it cannot be seen as a fair or level playing field. Albany had several community leaders who pushed to find government programs to fill this gap. After all the interviews, the bank offered me the job, and I accepted the opportunity. Banking was a job I wanted. I recalled Psalm 37:4 (take delight in the Lord and he will give you your heart's desire.

After I was hired, I began the 18-month comprehensive training program as a management trainee. I was excited to be given this new opportunity. As a management trainee, I will be trained in every job in the bank including: teller service, customer service, back office loan administration & deposit administration, financial analysis, retail & commercial lending, mortgage lending, specialized lending, private banking and branch management. Yes, a lot to cover in 18-months. There were five of us in the training program, myself and four other young men, three white and one other black guy. We all got along well. In fact, we developed a bond. Although there was some racial diversity, noticeably absent from our group were women. However, it was just good to see some diversity. I was glad to see another black guy in the program alongside me. This guy was from Atlanta, a recent Morehouse graduate, who was newly married, with no children. He had temporarily relocated to Albany to complete the training program because there was an opening in the internship here. His plan was to complete the program and then be placed in a job with the company in Atlanta where he would re-join his wife, who was still living and working in Atlanta. Throughout our training, the five of us often had to travel to the bank's headquarters in Atlanta to attend bank classes. One thing Atlanta was and still is famous for is its entertainment and nightlife. So, we young guys, in our early twenties, we're looking to have fun and relax after classes while in the City. In order to be fair, we decided to alternate, allowing each person to choose what we would do for entertainment during our trips to Atlanta. I am a big sports fan. So when it was my night to choose, we usually went to a sporting event, like a Hawks game. When it was time for the other to choose the entertainment, they usually selected a gentlemen's clubs for us to attend. On one evening, when it was my choice, we attended an Atlanta Hawks game and saw a matchup with the Hawks and Bulls. We saw Dominique Wilkens and Michael Jordan square off in a terrific game.

BETTER THAN GOOD TO BE GREAT

Training in the Program

The expectations were high not only from others but also from me. I not only wanted to be successful but I wanted to excel, be a star in the program. Being one of two black trainees in the program, I felt I had to be better that my white counter parts just to get equal consideration. Allow me to be clear. None of my supervisors expressed or made me feel I had to be better just to be equal. But it was the pressure I felt from inside of my own making. This feeling was of my own volition, which was probably based on some of my experiences, and had nothing to do with how I was treated by my superiors at the bank. I fact, most of them were nothing less than cordial and receptive to me. Now, whether it was true, that I had to better just to be equal, I cannot say. Regardless, it was the course of action I thought was required for my success. Therefore, I delved deep within myself to discover that inner drive. KD and I would have discussions about how we need to conduct ourselves as we navigated through the program. My philosophy was we had to put in the extra time and work just to be on equal ground as the white trainees. Whenever we were given the directive to be at work by 8 o'clock, I would make it a point to arrive by 7, or at the very latest, 7:30. I believed that being early is equivalent to being on time, whereas being on time is equivalent to being late. KD typically showed up at work sometime between 8:00 and 8:30. Whenever I confronted him, he would consistently reply by stating that white individuals are allowed to get away with it, and we should be given the same privilege. On this particular matter, he and I would frequently engage in arguments.

My contention was that the scrutiny of black trainees like us was intensified, making it seem like a much bigger deal when we didn't meet the mark. Additionally, regardless of the accuracy of my assessment, it is imperative that our actions are not influenced by the choices made by others. One thing I always do is hold myself accountable to choosing a path of excellence. My commitment to maintaining a high level of work ethic and my desire to produce tangible results were unwavering. I made a conscious effort to exceed expectations and go the extra mile on every task that I was given. I put in a lot of effort to make sure I completed everything thoroughly. I put in the additional time to help out other areas after completing my assignments. My intention was to fully utilize the learning opportunity and make the most of the training by gaining as much knowledge as possible. If I'm being honest, deep down, I viewed my fellow trainees as my competitors. My goal was to be the most remarkable person in the entire group. I always strived for their well-being and offered my help whenever possible. I worked really hard to reach my full potential.

The fact that this was noticed by those who were supervising me is worth mentioning. Following the completion of the 18-month program, I was given the opportunity to work for the bank. All five of us did not complete the program. When everything was said and done, there were only three individuals left - myself, KD, and another trainee. Despite the fact that two other trainees did not complete the 18-month program, KD, my fellow trainee, was given the opportunity to repeat nine months of the program because of their unsatisfactory performance review. One of the contributing factors to him being asked to repeat a section of the program was the debate we had about certain actions and whether they were acceptable or not. KD was very upset. Throughout the program, he had been eagerly awaiting the moment when he would finally be able to secure a full-time job, return to Atlanta, and be reunited with his wife. Reluctantly, he initially accepted the nine months repeat of a portion of the program because his only other option was to be terminated. I made a deliberate attempt to support him and convince him of the value of staying the course and seeing the program through to its completion. My desire was for him to not let this temporary setback lead him into making permanent decisions about his future plans. The pride and the embarrassment of not finishing the program in the initial 18 months got the best of him, so he quit about six weeks later and retuned to Atlanta to look for another job.

BANKING CULTURE, MERGERS, BUYOUTS AND ACQUISITIONS

I learned early on what banking culture involved. In my first five years of working at the bank, I had worked for four different banks without leaving the company. First, we bought a bank and changed our name. Then we were acquired by a larger bank and our name was changed. Then we went through a sequence of acquiring several banks across the nations and changed our name once again. The beginning of my career afforded me the opportunity to learn how to make loan decisions on my own. The company grew to become a large super conglomerate bank, with offices all over the United States and eventually through the world. In fact, at that time the bank became the second largest bank in the United States.

As the bank grew, individual loan officers were given less autonomy in making credit decisions for approving or denying loans. Decisions became more automated, based on a scoring system. This loan evaluation process was perhaps efficient from the banking operational perspective; however, it didn't always prove to be effective in serving the credit needs of the local customers. Recognizing this issue, corporate bank officials implemented limited overrides to allow exceptions to be made to the scoring system. In other words, if the system denied a loan request, the loan officer could override the system's decisions by providing written justification for the exception. The exceptions had to be kept to a minimum because if the exceptions were made too often, then it was no longer regarded as an exception but rather a normal practice and negate the effectiveness of the policy. The bank examiners kept a close watch on this process to ensure that there was no disparaging treatment of customers. The larger the bank grew, the fewer exceptions were allowed. I understood the reason for the loan scoring system. The scoring process was implemented to ensure that all loans were judged based on the same criteria, which was intended to promote fairness and equality in making loan decisions. There was a problem with only implementing a scoring system. If you had a group of people who were disenfranchised as a result of being denied access to capital and assets in the past, the scoring process does not close the inherent gap of those who have never had the opportunity to get the necessary capital to qualify in the scoring matrix.

My First Position after the Training

After completing the training program, I was assigned the assistant branch manager job at one of the local branches. This was a period of growth and continued learning.

As an assistant branch manager, I went to regional bank meetings from time to time. One of the other interns, who completed the program with me, was working as the assistant branch manager of another branch. He and I bonded, and he became not just another co-worker, but I considered him a good friend. We frequently rode together to the out-of-town meetings, alternating driving to the meetings. On one occasion that I drove, the meeting was about a half hour away. We had a very interesting conversation about not only banking but also about race relations in our community. My friend was white; he was raised in South Georgia, attended a private school, and was a down-to-earth guy. I apologized to him for my preconceived notion that because of his background, I thought he was snobbish and pretentious. Quite the contrary, he was just the opposite. He was down-to-earth and very pleasant to talk to. He talked to me about his time at the private school he attended. He spoke of how so many of his friends at his high school were racist. He told me that drugs of all kinds were prevalent at the school. I shared with him my experience of attending public school. I explained that racism was present in my school as well. We both acknowledged that it was a problem everywhere. After our bank meeting, we headed back to Albany. Driving back on a two-lane country road in South Georgia, I passed a Georgia State Trooper traveling in the opposite direction after I topped a hill. The officer made an immediate U-turn and began to follow me. The Patrolman turned on his lights. At that time, my friend asked, is he after you? I said yeah, he probably clocked me speeding. My friend asked me if I was speeding. I looked down at the speedometer and told him, *yeah, I was speeding.* Maybe, as I was coming down that hill, the car accelerated more than I realized. I slowed down, but it was too late. The officer had already clocked me with his radar, so I pulled over to the side of the road and stopped. The officer pulled behind me and sat in his car for several minutes. I rolled down my window and just waited. My friend said I'm glad you don't have any drugs in the car. I said what you mean, drugs in the car. He explained that most of his friends would have probably had some illegal drugs in their car, which would be a problem. I said, yeah, that would be a problem. I said *rest assured, there are no drugs in my car*. He said he knew I didn't have any drugs. He said being pulled over by the police made him nervous. He thought about previous situations when he had traveled with some of his other buddies, and they did have drugs in their car. I was very nervous as well, but for other reasons. I remember repeating to myself, stay calm and relax. The officer finally approached my car on the driver's side. The officer asked for my driver's license and registration. I told the officer that my license and registration were in the glove compartment of my car and that I would reach over and get them for him. As I reached to open my glove compartment, I watched the officer in my sideview mirror. He took two steps back, the gun still in his holster; he never pulled the weapon, and he just put his hand on the gun. Very nervously, I made sure I moved very slowly. I gave the officer my license and registration. He asked me where I was coming from and where I was going in such a hurry. I explained to him that I was a manager with a bank in Albany and was leaving a meeting in another town and returning to Albany. The officer said his radar clocked me at 67 miles an hour in a 55-mile-an-hour zone. I explained to him that I didn't realize I was going that fast. I told him that my car may have accelerated on me a little more than I realized as I topped the hill. The officer returned to his car for several more minutes. While we waited, my friend told me he was impressed with how you responded to that trooper. I asked him what he meant by that. He said he was so impressed that I thought I would announce to the officer and describe exactly how to get my license and registration. He said he never would have thought to say that to the officer. I told my friend that he didn't think about that because he was not black. He asked me what I meant by that. I told him as a black man, I have to think carefully about those situations, and even then, sometimes that's not enough. I explained to him that as a black man, white police officers tend to be more likely to be suspicious of me simply because of the color of my skin. I described to him the world that I live in. I told my friend that he never had to look at life situations through the eyes of a black man. I told him the view from my lenses is very different from his. He said, I never thought about that, but he understands. He clarified that he respected me even more, considering what I must consider. These were things he said he never had to think about. He shared with me that he and his girlfriend were conversing about me. He said she had commented about me, which she thought was a compliment. She made the statement that I was really smart and nice for a black guy. He asked her what she meant by "for a black guy." He said he told her I was smart, articulate, and nice for any guy, white or black.

He told me that he explained to her that she was wrong to insinuate that black people weren't usually smart and kind. He went on to say that he told her she shouldn't say things like that because that is stereotyping and a racist statement. As we continued this conversation, he mentioned that his grandfather felt the way his girlfriend did about black people. He told me he wanted me to meet his grandfather. He said that his grandfather had preconceptions that were wrong concerning black people. He wanted his grandfather to meet me to help change his perception of black people. Somewhat reluctantly, I agreed to go with him to meet his grandfather. He told me that he wanted to change his grandfather's racist thinking by introducing him to me. His grandfather was a retired wealthy businessman. He was very active in the community, a chamber of commerce member, and a board of directors on several prominent community organizations. I do appreciate my co-worker and friend for his attempts to change his grandfather's way of thinking. I believe he was truly sincere in his motives.

Desiring Acceptance

My friend arranged a meeting for us to go and visit his grandfather. Although his grandfather was retired, he did consultant work and maintained an office. My friend and I met his grandfather at his office. We went into the office, and my friend introduced me. After I was introduced, I felt I was being interviewed by the retired businessman. He begins with a barrage of questions. Where are you from? Who are your parents? Where did you attend high school? Where did you attend college? All of which I answered. Knowing what I knew about his racist mindset, initially, it was hard for me not to be offended by what appeared to be his interrogation. However, I settled down and accepted it simply as him wanting to get to know me and my background. I realized that it was just as important for me to allow him the opportunity to get to know me as it was for me to get to know him without stereotyping. After visiting for about an hour, we started to leave the office. His grandfather stopped me at the door and said that he thought I was a fine young man and that meeting me was a pleasure. I replied likewise. Weeks later, my friend recalled our meeting with his grandfather and told me he likes me and thinks a lot of me. He went on to say his grandfather would ask about me from time to time. My friend said he could see small changes in his grandfather, or "gramps," as he called him.

PROMOTION BRINGS
RESENTMENT

Having the opportunity does not guarantee success. There were those on both sides of the racial divide who did not support me as a banker.

After completing the training program, my first job assignment was that of an assistant branch manager and loan officer. One of my first challenges was to contend with the resentment of some employees who did not like being supervised by me. I want to emphasize that not all employees liked me as their supervisor, but some did not initially like me being their supervisor. They were upset about being managed by a young man who had been with the company less than two years, while many of them had been with the company for more than 15 or 20 years. Some of the staff were open and transparent about how they felt and told me they were insulted. They told me they felt the company had betrayed them because they had a hand in training me, only to have me become their supervisor months later. They were angry that they were not given a chance to be promoted to a management position. Knowing how they felt about this situation kept me on my toes. I knew it would be easy for those who resented me to set me up for failure if I didn't stay sharp and know my job well. I knew I had to find a way to gain their trust. Suffice it to say, I worked hard, worked smart, and watched my back. By the same token, I understood that in order to gain their trust, I had to empathize with them. I had to try to understand what they were feeling. I showed them that I cared and was concerned about their progress with the company. So, I was considerate of them and allowed them privileges and freedoms as an incentive for doing a good job.

I understood that I needed to gain their trust. If they performed well in their job assignments, then they would be successful. If they were successful, then I was successful. As a result, I gained favor with them, and they worked hard to make the bank branch succeed, which reflected well on me and helped me to advance. I emphasized teamwork. I was the leader, but we began and finished as a team. I realized the employees who expressed resentment towards me weren't angry with me, but rather, they were upset with the company for not giving them the opportunity they felt they deserved. I got them to realize that part of my job as their manager was to provide them the opportunity to advance and support them in their endeavors. My philosophy as a manager is to do my job well by training my staff and equipping them with the necessary means to be promoted. I vowed to them that I would help them advance in the company if they continued to work hard to promote its mission. I wanted to give them the same opportunity that was afforded me.

Winning the trust of clients presented more than a challenge. There were times when some white clients of the bank would refuse to allow me to assist them with their banking requests because I am black. I'm sure it happened more times than I knew about. I felt that these incidents were not isolated to the southern part of the country; however, I believe they are just more prevalent. I can only speak to the dozens of times that I recognized it, or someone told me that the customer refused to allow me to assist them. I remember once, while I was the assistant branch manager on the northwest side of town, a white man walked into the bank. This was a relatively quiet morning as far as foot traffic in the bank. Only two loan officers, the branch manager and me, were at our location. This particular morning, the branch manager was out of the office. A middle-aged white man, a longtime bank customer, walked in and asked the customer service representative if he could speak to a loan officer. Sitting in my office, I had my door open. I could see people in the lobby and hear their conversation.

The representative responded to the man's request very politely and professionally. She told the customer to allow me to introduce you to our assistant branch manager, Mr. Williams; he will gladly take care of whatever you need. Hearing her statement, I stood at my desk to walk out of my office and introduce myself. Just as I stood up, I heard him say him and point towards me. She replied, *yes, sir. Mr. Williams is our assistant branch manager; he can help you with any credit request you may have.* He shook his head. He then asked if there was anyone else he could talk to. She explained that the only other loan officer was the branch manager, who was out of the office at the time. She reiterated to him that I was more than capable of assisting him with any loan request he had. He responded by saying that's okay, as he left the bank, giving me a glaring look of disgust. The CSR stood frozen in place, her face flushed red with embarrassment. She looked at me and said she was so sorry that it happened. I returned to my office and sat down at my desk. She walked into my office. She declared that this type of attitude has no place in society. I agreed with her, but I also told her that she need not apologize for the ignorance of others.

Rejection is always disappointing, but I was prepared for it because I had dealt with it before. I was prepared for not being accepted by who didn't look like me, people of a different race. I remember being warned before I was hired. I was not as prepared for the support of some people within the black community. Don't get me wrong, more often than not, countless people from the black community rallied to support me, to whom I am extremely grateful. Many of them were supporters and cheerleaders for me. They were the ones who called me to encourage me and tell me they appreciated my efforts and what I was doing. They wanted to see me help make a difference. They told me they understood the challenges and the pressure I faced daily. There was also the other side of the road. Some even said to me that I would not succeed in a banking career in South Georgia. I understood what they were saying. They encouraged me to leave this small town and move to a larger city where there was more diversity, more people would support me, and I would grow more rapidly as a banker. I knew there was more opportunity in larger metropolitan areas with more diversity, like in Atlanta. I knew it would be challenging and daunting at times. But, I felt a need. I saw a niche.

I thought that maybe, just maybe, I could make a difference here at home, where I was afforded this opportunity. I was motivated. For my detractors, I harbored no ill feelings towards them. To all the naysayers for the lack of faith in me and my ability, I have no adverse judgments against them. In fact, I'm somewhat grateful for them doubting me. When people told me I would not be successful, they helped me be more determined. They gave me drive. They helped me to develop an inward motivation. I pushed myself with a feeling that I would not be denied. I wanted to work as hard as I needed to be successful. I was willing to do whatever it took to prove myself to be the best.

All in all, I was driven to do it the right way, with integrity. Under no circumstances was I willing to sacrifice sound morals and integrity to be successful. I just wanted to make it happen. This drive was not to prove to others that I could be successful. It was to prove to myself that I could achieve a level of success. You should never pursue something to prove yourself to others because if that's your motive, you have given others the key of approval to determine whether or not you are successful. If you give others the key, you cannot determine if your outcome is productive or successful. Always work to prove things to yourself, not others, so that you control the determination of your success. If others have control, you will always be dependent and at the mercy of others to give you a feeling of satisfaction or achievement. So, maintain control and only work to prove things to yourself.

During my banking career, I received periods of accelerated promotion favor. This favor, I believe, was orchestrated by God. In order to make things happen for me, God placed people in my life to help direct my destiny. One of these people was my supervisor early in my career. I would describe her as a southern belle. She was a woman who spoke with a little bit of that southern twang, short in stature but an absolute fireball of energy. A woman who worked her way up in banking after beginning her career as a teller, she understood what overcoming resistance and roadblocks to success was like.

Similarly, the plight of a woman in corporate America reflected the same challenges as blacks or African Americans. She was, indeed, a progressive thinker who worked to remove barriers in order to create opportunity. All I needed was a chance to succeed and not be boxed into a limited position, a position without a glass ceiling. In order to win the game, you have to be in the game. Yes, all I needed was a chance, a seat at the table. I thought of Proverbs 18:16, A man's gift makes room for him and brings him before great men. My supervisor introduced me to people I would describe as movers and shakers in the community. These were prominent people who made decisions and influenced the direction of society. This interaction was monumental for my development as a twenty-three-year-old developing banker. I learned the importance of networking and how it guided success.

I gradually worked through the banking system, first as an assistant branch manager and then as a branch manager. During that time as branch manager, I did retail and commercial lending. My last branch manager position was with the largest branch in the city. There were 24 branch personnel under my supervision. My staff included several retail or consumer loan officers, the branch teller operation, and a central money vault for all the bank's Southwest Georgia branches. I managed the main office for three years. It was there that I learned how to manage stress. I learned how to deal with the good, the bad, and the ugly. After a few years of managing the main office, I accepted the position in the commercial lending department as the small business lending manager for the city.

LADY

One client was a woman I met early in my banking career. I called her Lady. Lady, eccentric, unusual, and yet one of the most fascinating people I have ever met. I met her in 1990. She and I would develop a very close relationship, not only as a banker but also as a friend and confidant. Lady was an attractive woman with red hair that was always neatly done. An extremely vain woman, early in our relationship, Lady would not allow me to enter to see her without having her hair and makeup freshen up. She was in her late 60s or early 70s when I met her. She was a former Miss America contestant. She was a self-made woman, a prominent real estate investor who managed her properties. She had amassed quite a bit of wealth and was not shy about letting anyone know she was a multi-millionaire.

Nevertheless, she owned a fortune in real estate. She was a very fierce businessperson who was outspoken and demanding. She was feisty. She had a raspy voice with a bit of a southern country drawl, and she could curse with the best of them or the worst of them, depending on how you looked at it. She described herself as being raised as an orphan. She told me that she was abandoned by her mother and raised by relatives who neglected and abused her. Because of this background, I believe she had developed a soft spot for people who were disenfranchised, outcast, or less fortunate. Along with her drive to be a successful businesswoman, she also wanted to be a champion for those who didn't have much money.

Good Deeds

In the early 1960s, racism was blatant, and explicit racial tension was high in the United States. Well, to date, we continue to struggle with the same issues. Lady told me about an incident that happened to her that changed her life forever.

As Lady explained it to me, here's what happened. She was riding one evening when she came upon a young black woman who appeared homeless. She called for the woman to come over to her car. She noticed that the woman was pregnant. The woman appeared to be homeless. Lady took the woman home with her and gave her a place to stay. During her stay with Lady, she gave birth to a baby boy. Since the woman had no means of caring for herself or a child, Lady offered the woman assistance in raising the child. As it turned out, Lady wound up raising the child herself. Having no children of her own, she fell in love with the baby boy and was proud to raise him as her own. Lady described to me how much she loved the child. She laughed about how hard it was for her to change his diapers. As a parent, I certainly could relate. Although she never legally adopted the child, she considered him to be her son. Lady did her very best to provide all the advantages that would allow him to experience the best life had to offer. She sent him to a private catholic school and then to a private college.

Lady told me that she never legally adopted him; however, she treated him like he was her own. As you can imagine, a white woman raising an African American child was not popular in the 1960s, especially in racially charged Albany, Georgia, one of the focuses of racial injustice during the civil rights movement. Lady talked about how she

52

would get looks, stares, glares, and comments from white people when they were with her in public. She told me the story of being in a grocery store once, and the cashier asked her why she had that little monkey with her. Lady told me that after cussing her out, she demanded that someone go and get the manager. When the manager arrived, she told him what the cashier said. Lady also told him how she did not ever want to see that cashier in the store again. She explained that she was a regular shopper in that store and had enough money to buy the store. One thing you need to know about Lady is that she never hesitated to let you know how much money she had. Also, she was not in the least bit shy about telling you off or giving you a piece of her mind. Lady raised the child, providing for him and giving him everything she thought he needed or wanted. She never wanted him to go lacking for anything. Suffice it to say, she admitted that she spoiled him as she would have had he been her biological child. She told me she wanted to ensure he was raised and afforded the things she never got as a child. He is a down-to-earth person. He has never been pompous, arrogant, or ostentatious in any way. In fact, like Lady, he has always done things to help those with less.

THE CONTROLLER

How I Met Lady

I got a phone call at the bank one morning from a young man telling me he was in Atlanta at a car dealership. He had seen a new Lexus that he wanted to buy. He explained that he would trade the BMW he had financed with our bank and buy the Lexus. So, he requested that I wire the money to the Lexus dealership, and he would come into the bank the following day and sign the loan documents. Before I could honor a request like this, I needed to be assured that I could secure the title for the new car and know that the person making the request was not trying to pull a fast one on me and never showed up to sign the loan documents. So, I asked my bank co-workers if they knew this guy. They all said yes, he is a regular client and the adopted son of "Lady." They explained that Lady was a wealthy, long-time client of the bank. I went back to the phone to speak to the guy, and he said to call Lady, and she would take care of the request. I called Lady, and after strongly proclaiming for several minutes that the guy didn't need a new car, she told me to go ahead and finance the car, and she would vouch for the new car.

She told me that if need be, I could go into her checking account and place a hold on the amount needed to secure the car purchase. There was enough money in the checking account to pay for the car twenty times over. The guy did just as he said he would and came into the bank the next day and signed the loan documents. Several months after the car was financed, I got a call from Lady. She was upset with the guy and wanted me to withdraw the funds from her checking account, pay off the loan balance, and bring the title to her. She explained that this would give her control because the title would be in her possession. However, it seemed like a win for the guy because he kept the Lexus and no longer had to make any payments. But this was just a way for her to feel she was in control.

Lady felt she could control everything and everybody. She felt empowered because she was wealthy. As kind-hearted as she was, she was somewhat of a manipulator. She used her money to get people to do for her. If she liked you, she loved you and would do anything for you.

On the other hand, if you ever did anything to cross her, she would be done with you. She was suspicious of people and, most often, rightfully so. People often wanted to get close to her because they were in some way after her money. I recall her telling me about people who would come by to visit. She told me that some of her visitors didn't care about her and that they were just after her money. So, she would just play along. Often time she was right.

INDECENT PROPOSAL

In my drive to succeed, I was determined not to allow myself to be taken in by illegal or ill-gotten gain. There's always someone around who will try to show you how to make some fast money. Be cautious, and don't get taken in by schemes and underhanded dealings. I was not one to push the envelope to see how far I could take a situation. That would always lead to trouble. Doing things the right way goes a long way. In a haste to expedite their careers and growth, there are those who allow themselves to be overtaken by temptation and put themselves in precarious situations. That spells trouble. These circumstances usually lead to terminations, embarrassment, public humiliation, and, in some cases, incarceration. There is no substitution for integrity and preserving a good name.

Proverbs 22:1 says that a good name is more desirable than great riches; to be esteemed or respected is better than silver or gold. People are often overtaken by temptation through greed and the love of money. Most of us are familiar with the scripture, 1st Timothy 6:10, which says, "For the love of money is a root of all kinds of evil. Some people, eager for money, have wandered from the faith and pierced themselves with many griefs. Several colleagues had fallen prey to unethical and illegal schemes that cost them their careers, and some even went to prison. I made a conscious effort and a priority to steer clear of those kinds of situations. I did, however, have several situations or proposals that were presented to me that I avoided. One in particular involved a well-known businessman who offered me a large sum of money to do something illegal. I was not about to consider doing anything against the law, no matter how much money he offered to pay me. This situation involved a client of mine, who was a respected and well-to-do businessman throughout the South. He owned a few multi-million dollar businesses. He came from a family who had tens of millions of dollars. He called me one day and asked me to come by to see him at his place of business. When I arrived at his office, he told me he had a proposition for me. He went on to say that this proposition could earn me hundreds of thousands of dollars. He explained that he had been appointed executor of a relative's estate, estimated to be worth between 80 to 100 million. However, he had become estranged from this relative and other members of his family. This had resulted in this relative, who was now in his 90s, changing his will and placing one of his siblings as executor of the estate. He went on to say that this relative's accounts were held at my bank, and the most recently dated will was in a file at my bank. He told me he would be willing to pay 100 thousand dollars to someone if that file could get lost. He said files get lost all the time. He went on to say that if the file with the most recent will gets lost, then the previous file that shows him to be the executor would be the most recent, which would make him the executor of the estate. I told him that if he had asked me to dispose of or destroy a legal document, there was no way I was willing to do that. He went further and offered 250 thousand if I could somehow facilitate the file disappearing. I clarified to him that I would not accept a million dollars to commit a crime. I told him I would leave his office and pretend we never had that conversation. After this encounter, I knew he was corrupt, and I no longer wanted to have any business dealings with him because he could not be trusted. When someone shows you that they are dishonest, deceitful, and unlawful, separate yourself from them. This will save you from so much grief and misery later on.

INTEGRITY DEALINGS

As a banker, I wanted to build relationships with reputable clients. When I considered developing a relationship with a client, I measured them using the five Cs of credit. The first of the five Cs of credit is character. This client obviously lacked character. So, he was crossed off my list for any further consideration of business dealings. Most of my clients were of good character with high moral standards.

Businessman from Massachusetts

These clients were great to work with. Developing relationships is the lifeline of a successful banker. One of my commercial clients was with a businessman from Massachusetts by way of Florida. I recall the first time I met him. He walked into the bank wearing a colorful button-up shirt with a tropical print and slacks - with a fresh tan, looking like he had just left the beach. He wore a gold necklace, gold bracelets, and rings on both hands. As a businessman, he was undoubtedly an unconventional dresser. He was dressed for relaxation. I don't recall seeing him in a coat and tie through all the years of doing business with him. He always dressed in casual attire. He loved bright, festive colors. Even the colors he painted the buildings of his businesses were always bright and festive. He said that festive colors set the tone for a cheerful attitude.

With his briefcase in hand, speaking with a distinct Bostin accent, he walked up to me, introduced himself, and told me he had purchased the skating ring across the street and wanted to open an account. I'll call him Mr. D. Mr. D owned several businesses. He owned multiple businesses in Georgia, Florida, and South Carolina. He kept a diverse business portfolio. Mr. D's diverse portfolio business model was designed to help him withstand the various ups and downs of the economy. When the economy surges, his real estate developments would be very profitable, and so would his other lines of business. A stern and crafty businessman, nevertheless, Mr. D was a super nice guy.

Mr. D and I often took road trips to South Carolina and central Georgia to visit some of his businesses. During those road trips, we had lots of discussions about business and his future plans. We also talked about life, family, and relationships. He and I developed a connection beyond just a banker-client relationship. We were friends. Every year around my birthday, he would send me one of his high-end cars to drive over the weekend. I'd get a phone call from him telling me he was filling one of his cars with gas, having the car detailed and sent to me to drive over the weekend. A few times, it was his cherry red Cadillac RX7 hard top convertible, a two-seater. That car was sweet. Needless to say, I really enjoyed driving that car.

Mr. D loved his family. Everything he did was centered on ensuring his family was happy and cared for. There is a saying that a good, strong woman is behind every successful man. That certainly holds true with his wife, Mrs. D., who was indeed a jewel of a woman who supported her husband. Two of Mr. D's most essential business principles were hard work and cleanliness. He demanded that all of his businesses be kept immaculately clean and organized. He even made sure the contractors kept the construction sites of his real estate developments neat and orderly at all times. That's a task that's not easily achieved.

Mr. D cared about people. He believed in treating people the way he wanted to be treated. Don't get me wrong, he was a stickler for hard work and getting the job done correctly. In fact, at times, he was pretty intense. He pushed his workers for successful results. He would get upset and chew them out, the staff and employees, even his family, if they failed to do their job effectively. Although caring, he was all business when it came down to work. His focus was customer satisfaction. His philosophy was to work hard, make some money, and have fun doing it.

Heart Breaking Tragedy

My cell phone rang on a Saturday afternoon. I was traveling home from a church men's retreat. The call was from one of Mr. D's business partners. He simply said that Mr. D died. I remember feeling as if all the air had been sucked out of the vehicle I was riding in. It was a surreal moment. I asked him what happened. He said he was not sure of the details but that his son had found him at his home earlier that morning, deceased. When I got to my house late that evening, I called Mr. D's son to express my deepest condolences and to tell him that I was available to support the family in any way needed. I told him to let me know if he needed me to do anything for them. He thanked me and explained the events leading to his finding his father. The following day, Sunday, my wife and I went to the house to see the family. Mrs. D asked me if I would do the eulogy at the funeral. She said Mr. D was very fond of me and considered me his spiritual leader. She went on to say she was sure that he would want me to be the one to pay tribute to him as his service. I told her that I would be honored.

Changing Banks

I had been in banking for eleven years and practically had a relationship with Lady from the beginning. There were ups and downs, successes and struggles. I had built quite a few business as well as personal relationships in the small city of approximately one hundred thousand people at that time. I was one of only a handful of black bank officers in the city and was the only commercial banker at any bank in the city. The other banks in town saw a need for diversity in their bank. They recognized the need for a black person to work for them to attract the growing number of black businesses in the area. As a result, I was getting job offers from other banks consistently. These meetings with other banks were very discrete. In the banking industry, if it becomes known that you are potentially leaving your current bank employer to work for another bank, your current employer would more than likely terminate you immediately, for fear of you actively transferring your existing portfolio of loan customers to the bank you are going to work for. Each time I got a call from another bank, I talked to them to see what they offered. My consideration for making a change was more than just based on money. I considered myself to be a young, upwardly mobile banker. I had the education and the training and was gaining more and more experience. So, when I sat down to talk about different jobs and positions, I was more interested in opportunities for advancement and not just a larger salary. The question I asked at the interview was centered on, after I am successful in the position I'm being hired for, what would be considered as my next move upward? The answers they gave were usually politically correct. I had to look closely at each job offer, investigate the work environment at that bank, and read between the lines. Some of the jobs offered higher salaries; however, most were lateral moves to a different bank doing the same job I was currently doing, with little promise of future advancement opportunities. I never accepted a job offer to go to another bank based exclusively on a salary increase.

After entertaining various offers over several weeks, I decided to leave a large multi-billion dollar bank and work for a small credit union. Many would measure this as a mistake, a bad decision on my part. I admit it certainly sounds like a mistake on the surface. I was leaving a multi-billion dollar financial institution with bank offices worldwide to work for a small 250-million dollar credit union with only six branch offices in Southwest Georgia. The difference is I was offered the opportunity to help start a commercial loan department and a chance to help write policies and grow as the institution grew. The plan for the credit union was to change the charter in a couple of years from a credit union to a bank. That was a process I wanted to be a part of. This was an opportunity for me to grow and deepen my bank experience. I felt this endeavor would expand my horizon in the banking industry. This would give me additional knowledge and experience, which would increase my value in the banking market. My goal is to one day become president and chief executive officer. This offer was indeed a growth opportunity in which I was looking forward to participating.

People don't always keep their word.

When this financial institution hired me, I was told I would come over as Vice President, the same title I had with my previous employer. I was also told that I was being brought in to help lead the new and developing commercial loan department and grow that department. These agreements are what attracted me to the position. As I mentioned, money was not the biggest driver for my decisions at this stage in my career. Although I was offered a larger salary, that was not my emphasis. I wanted to be a part of the foundation of something growing into something larger than just a regular job. These were the things promised to me and certainly the most important job attributes to get me to accept the position. I was told by the top executive at the institution that they had hired a young guy who only had a little banking experience at that time and had just completed a commercial training program at another bank. He was going to lead the commercial loan department. It just so happened that this person was a close relative to the CEO. The CEO told me his vision was for me to come in and work alongside this person and share my years of experience to help develop and grow the department. The plan was to change the charter from a credit union to a regional bank in a few years. This was the opportunity I had been searching for. I left the multibillion-dollar national bank and took the job with the smaller 250-million-dollar credit union. I was excited and looking forward to the challenge of being on the ground floor of a growing financial institution.

When I got to the credit union and began working, it was immediately apparent that my co-worker had a different acceptance of the idea of the two of us working side by side to build the commercial department. I remember the first meeting we had after I got there. The CEO said I'm looking for you guys to develop the department together. He told everyone that I had a lot of commercial bank experience and could offer a lot of guidance. He emphasized that he wanted us to work together as co-leaders of the department. My co-worker was never receptive to us being equal partners in leading the department. I noticed that my counterpart's title was Assistant Vice President, which was understandable because he had just completed commercial bank training and needed more experience. I had been at the credit union for about a month when the CEO called me to his office. With the co-worker present, he said that he wanted to change my title from Vice President to Assistant Vice President because the vision was for us to work together as co-partners. He said this would not be the case if my title reflected a higher level than that of my co-worker. He did say that my salary would not be reduced, but he just wanted us to have equal titles. Of course, this was disconcerting to me. It was a direct reversal of what was promised to me when I left the bank to come to work for the credit union. Although this was upsetting, I accepted this change. After all, I'm still in the position to work on the foundation of something that would grow into something much bigger. I used it to inspire me rather than get upset and try to fight the situation. I remained motivated.

As we worked together, my co-worker came across several challenging loan proposals that he and I discussed. I advised him of the high inherent risk involved in some of the proposals. I suggested that we take a more secure conservative approach since we were a small department and just getting started with our portfolio. I suggested using the support from the Government's Small Business Administration (SBA) to guarantee a portion of the loan to mitigate our risk and limit our potential for loss. I had experience facilitating SBA loans with my previous employer. So, after I got to the credit union, I successfully submitted the necessary applications to the Small Business Administration to get the credit union accepted into the SBA loan program. For various reasons that he gave, he didn't take my advice in many situations. He felt it was too long of a process and too much paperwork. Against my advice, he made a loan of several hundred thousand dollars to a start-up business to someone with no experience in that line of business, and the collateral was only inventory that was not properly valued. Less than a year later, this furniture store business was bankrupt, and we were faced with those losses. Several other high-risk loan situations came up in which my advice was not taken, and as a result, we had to work our way out of losses. There was resistance from my co-leader to take my advice and suggestions. Why do you think that was the case? He was allowed to proceed with some high-risk loan requests without much, if any, advice from me. This made me feel that my input was unwanted.

Nevertheless, I remained motivated. Please understand that credit losses are not unusual in banking. They happen all the time. It's just a matter of managing the losses, protecting the institution's capital position, and not jeopardizing its solvency. I also want to point out that the institution was doing very well financially. My point is that my role and importance were downplayed or reduced.

The institution's assets and capital position grew, surpassing goals and expectations. The company added branch offices and expanded internal departments to support its growth. The commercial department added several new commercial officers and support staff as well. The plan for applying to change the charter to a regional bank was full steam ahead. The charter change was successful, and the institution became a regional bank.

DON'T BOX ME IN

All the roles, titles, and positions were increasing except mine. A new corporate main office was built on the Northwest side of town. When plans were made to move into the new corporate building, I was told I would not be moving. Instead, I would remain at the downtown location. They wanted me to continue to manage my commercial portfolio and serve as branch manager of the downtown location, which was a designated low-to-moderate income area and predominately black area of town. Don't get me wrong, I was perfectly happy serving the black community; in fact, that was part of my mission. I thought there was no reason I couldn't do that while sitting at the big table in the corporate building.

I felt my role was being minimized. I was being boxed into a limited role. I was frustrated. I felt that my loyalty, hard work, and dedication were not being rewarded. The impulsive thing would have been quitting and finding another job at another bank. After all, I had been pursued by several banks in town, and landing another job would not have been hard. But I prayed about it, and the answer I received was to stay where I was. The message I received was to dig deep into my determination, stay motivated, and press for success in my current situation. Like a flower planted in difficult soil, I needed to stay where I was and blossom in my position. The confirmation in my spirit was that changing banks would not change my circumstances but would only change the bank where I was working.

I was certain I would have the same situation at any other bank in South Georgia. Once again, I could hear those words of the bank president who hired me and gave me my first job as a banker: "Albany is not a progressive city." I watched as other commercial loan officers who didn't look like me came in and advanced while I was being boxed in. Allow me to explain what I mean by being boxed in. Regardless of my education and experience, my superiors seem to want me to be confined to only serving clients in certain parts of the community. As I mentioned before, serving the minority community was a mission of mine. However, I wanted to be able to serve the entire diverse client base in the community.

I was reminded of King David in the bible. In the 16th chapter of the book of Samuel, David was appointed to be the leader. However, he was sent back into the field to tend the sheep after he was appointed. I imagine David felt some dismay. He probably felt he was supposed to simply move into the leadership role as he was selected. Instead, David was returned to the field until such time that he was to prove himself. During his return to the field to tend the sheep, the Lord was preparing him to be that mighty man of valor. He was preparing him, laying the foundation for him to be the warrior he would have to be to be king. You see, while David was tending the sheep, he often had to fight off predators like lions and tigers to protect the sheep. I imagine the job of tending sheep taught David not only how to be a strong warrior but also that by going back into the field, he learned patience, tolerance, and endurance, all needed to be successful.

Similarly, although I didn't know it then, my struggle was my time back in the field. This was designed to help prepare me for success as a leader. Looking back on these events, I see that they were more than just grooming me for a job or career; they were preparing me for a calling in my life. Still being frustrated at times, I decided to trust the process.

Instead of leaving the bank, I reached deep inside and found that inward motivation to drive me to exceed my peers and their production. I continued to work harder and smarter. I was the first in the building and the last to leave every day, but the struggle continued. I grew my loan portfolio with almost no loan losses. My delinquency and charge-off ratio was well below the bank's established goals. I continued ramping up my calls on new business relationships to attract larger profitable companies and client relationships.

There was one relationship in particular that I recall. The owner had a multi-million dollar business. He was someone I was acquainted with and had a previous relationship with. In fact, he was the bank president that had given me my first banking job. The same person told me twenty years earlier that Albany was not a progressive community. He had retired from banking and had started his own company. We had a very good conversation. We spent time reminiscing and catching up on former co-workers. During my visit, I asked him if he would allow me to be his banker and move his banking relationship to my bank. He explained that he was very comfortable banking with one of my old co-workers as his banker. I told him that I perfectly understood. He said, however, that if he ever decided to change banks, I would be the person he would call. This multi-million dollar relationship would have proven to be a big account for me. I listed this visit on my weekly call report to the commercial department, informing everyone of my efforts and the potential for future business. Several months later, I got a call from him saying that his banker was retiring, and he was interested in moving his relationship over to my bank and would allow me to be his banker, just as he said he would. I was excited at the opportunity to land this big account. I called some of my bank executive officers and informed them I would get this account. The next day, my friend, the business owner, called me and said he had just received a visit from a couple of my bank executives. He told me they had come by to tell him they wanted him to request another banker to handle his relationship at our bank instead of me. He said he explained to them that he told me I had come by months earlier to ask for his business relationship, and he had promised to give it to me if he ever decided to move his relationship. He went on to say that he wanted me to know that he had kept his word to me and they were taking the relationship from me. A few hours later, those two bank executives walked into my office. They told me that they had paid a visit to my friend, the owner of the business, and told him that once he moved his relationship to our bank, it would be better serviced by another commercial banker. The justification they gave me for this decision was that this other banker was familiar with his business and could do a better job of serving him. I knew this was a totally bogus reason for not allowing me to manage this relationship. The two bank executives also said they appreciated my hard work and efforts to bring in the larger accounts and that I should continue pursuing relationships such as churches and small businesses in the community. I knew that I was being boxed in and held down. If I'm not given the opportunity to manage the larger relationships, then there is justification for them not paying me a higher salary like that of my co-workers. As commercial bank officers, we are rewarded for the relationships we bring into the bank. Growing our portfolio is the measure used to determine our salary, bonuses, and promotions. If they don't allow me to manage the larger relationships, I won't get the chance to earn the same salary as my counterparts. I was livid because I felt this was just another way to keep me from advancing to a higher level as a commercial banker. Once again, I was upset, but I dug deeper and became more determined. I was motivated.

EVEN IF THE STRUGGLE CONTINUES

Frustrated, I thought, what should I do? The way I saw it, I had two choices. The first choice would be to quit and go to another bank. Besides, in the past, I had been pursued by many other banks to work for them, right? However, if I were to change banks, I wouldn't find a similar situation where I have to fight through disparaging treatment by that bank. This was one of those forks in the road. I was convinced that the established viewpoint of black bankers in Albany and South Georgia, for that matter, was the same throughout. It was one of confinement and limitation. This stereotypical mindset supports what I was warned about years earlier at the beginning of my banking career. Albany, for the most part, was not a progressive community.

Don't get me wrong, I didn't believe this was the case in absolute terms, meaning 100 % across the board. I felt that this was the situation in the majority of establishments. The second choice would be for me to stay with this bank, dig deep within myself, and find the motivation to succeed. I prayed for an answer. In my spirit, I heard the Lord say to me to keep working where I am, and he will give me what I desire. I relied on an old truth: let the Lord fight my battles. God was teaching me perseverance. Sometimes, running away hampers your progress and delays your development in becoming the person you were called to be. Determined, I used this setback to ignite a hunger in me to show myself that I would not be denied. I continued to bank the small businesses and churches, helping them gain access to capital and grow into large businesses. I also landed several other large business relationships to add to my commercial loan portfolio.

Moving to the Big House

Don't think of people who don't like you, try to discredit you, and tear you down as your enemy. They are the ones pushing you into your place of success.

NOT JUST COINCIDENCES

Business Trip

God always works things for our good, even when we don't see them. His way is not like our way. Nevertheless, God is watching out for our well-being, and His grace and mercy cover us continually. Grace is God's gift, blessing us with what we don't deserve. On the other hand, mercy is God sparing us from what we deserve if justice had a free hand. In this game of life, it's not simply about us all the time. In other words, God sometimes will allow things to take place in our lives that will not only bless us but also exalt others in the process. We have to understand that God will do something for us, and as a result, it will trickle down and support the needs of so many other people. I saw this take place in a situation that happened to me.

Once, I took a business trip to Atlanta to visit a client. It was the middle of the week, on a Wednesday or Thursday.

I had planned to leave the office a little early because I didn't want to get caught in that evening's Atlanta traffic. But as fate would have it, I had things to delay me, and I didn't get to leave until around 3 o'clock. Leaving Albany to make that approximately 3-hour drive to Atlanta, I was stressed because I knew I would get caught in the Atlanta traffic. To make matters worse, this was in the winter season, and the daylight hours were shorter. Traveling on Interstate 75 at around 5:30 PM, my truck began to lose power. No matter how much I tried to accelerate, the truck was going slower and slower. I thought to myself, my transmission is going out. And wouldn't you know it, I was on a stretch of the interstate where there was no town and no operating service station or convenience store. Also, it was getting dark, and I dreaded being stranded on the side of the interstate at night. Forced to turn off on the next exit, I looked to the left and the right and saw an abandoned convenience store on each side of the exit. I drove a little ways after exiting, to see if I could find something open before I called Triple A to send a tow truck. After I passed one of the abandoned convenience stores, I saw a large brown warehouse with a spray-painted sign that said Rick's Garage and Transmission Service. I pulled in and asked Rick to examine my truck, and he confirmed that my transmission was shot. Rick told me he could replace my transmission but could only get one the next day. I told him that was fine and I needed to call for a rental car to pick me up. However, because of where I was, no rental car service would agree to come to pick me up. So, Rick offered to allow his assistant to drive me 20 miles to the nearest rental car service to rent a vehicle. Although a little late, I was able to arrive at the hotel on my client's property and attend the reception for his grand opening.

It was a blessing for my transmission to go out right there near the transmission repair shop. Some people may complain and say, *why wouldn't God allow your truck not to experience any problems? You would have made the trip and arrived home without incident.* Again, I will say that our way is not like God's way. God never said that we wouldn't experience tribulations. He simply said He would never leave or forsake us and would see us through the struggles. God allows us to go through things to develop and help us progress in many different areas. I'm beginning to understand that every situation is not exclusively about us. We can sometimes be selfish and think that everything is about our situation and we want it to be perfect without incident. That simple situation of my transmission going out when and where it did could have been used to help so many others outside of causing a slight inconvenience to me. It could have been that the owner of the transmission shop was having financial problems and had been praying for an increase in business. Or better yet, the people who sell automotive parts for the transmission needed a boost in business, or they may lose their home, car, or other financial difficulties. I could have been used to be a part of that process of helping a situation. Don't get me wrong, I don't know why that slight inconvenience happened; I'm simply saying things we go through involve more than just us. However, we can be assured that God will make provision for us in every situation.

TEST

I have always worked hard to be the very best provider for my family. For most of my life, I worked two jobs. For 18-years, I worked part-time as an adjunct accounting instructor at the College of Business at the university. At this time, I had been there for more than 13 years. Additionally, I have been in banking for more than 25 years. I always had a very sound work ethic. I was one of the first to arrive at work and one of the last ones to leave at the end of the day. I believed in giving my employer an honest day's work every day. I was a vice president of commercial lending and had been pretty successful doing my job. I made lots of contacts through networking and community involvement. I volunteered with many charitable nonprofit and civic organizations and, in most cases, held seats as a board of directors member. For many of the organizations, I was chairman of the board for some time. For several years, I served on the finance committee of the board of directors for the chamber of commerce. So, this involvement afforded me the opportunity to have quite a following in the community, which translated into having successful business contacts and clients for my jobs.

One of the bank's senior vice presidents asked me a question that caught me off guard. He asked me if I had done something to offend one of the executive vice presidents at the bank. I replied, no. In fact, I thought he and I got along well. I mentioned the two of us sometimes worked out at the same gym early mornings before work. My relationship with this EVP at the bank was both professional and cordial and certainly friendly. As far as I was concerned, we also had a good relationship away from the office. So, I asked him why he'd asked me that question. His reply floored me. He said, "He does not like you." So I asked, "What do you mean?" He went on to say that this executive had come to him on several occasions and made the statement that I should not even be in banking. So I asked him what reason he gave him for saying that about me. He said he never gave a reason. It just so happens that my supervisor told me about this. So, I asked my supervisor if there was a problem with my job performance or how I did my job, and his answer was no. In fact, he laughed about it. Bewildered, I asked again why he would come to him and say that about me. He grinds, shakes his head, and says he does not like you. Initially, I just brushed it off and said I wouldn't worry about it.

After all, I didn't report to him, so he can do nothing to me anyway. However, as I thought about it, he and I had to work together rather closely in many cases. So, I began to pray about it and asked the Lord what I should do to mend a relationship that was never broken from my vantage point. Despite his feelings toward me, the Lord told me to show him more love. My initial thought was, *Lord, if he does not like me, then that's his problem. Let him deal with it.* Then I heard that small voice inside me say, *show him more love anyway.* That's hard to do when you know someone dislikes you and maybe tries to undermine you and your success. The Lord reminded me that I'm always asking for spiritual and professional growth. If I were to achieve that growth, more would be required of me.

So, *I said, Okay, Lord, I will go out of my way to show him more genuine care and friendship.* That EVP and I worked in the same building, so I would make an extra effort to reach out to him and stop by his office at least once daily. I'd ask how he and his family were doing and offer to assist him with anything he needed that was work related or otherwise, just showing basic kindness. After about a month of reaching out to him, I said *Lord, I've been doing this now several times a week for a month. Isn't that enough?* Then that same voice inside of me said what you have done thus far is worthless because it's not coming from your heart. The Lord revealed to me that it was not coming from my heart because I kept counting how many times I'd reached out to him. God was teaching me that when we want to grow, the things we do must be from the heart. It's not simply our actions or going through the motions of doing something that brings about successful results. Sustainable growth or success is more about actions that come from your heart. So I continued to reach out to this person for more than a year, so much so until it was almost second nature, and I didn't realize I was showing him more and more kindness. It has become a part of me now. It was now what I did on a regular basis. It became so much a part of me that I was extending that same consideration approach to others. Now, that's growth. As a result, the Lord opened doors of promotion for me professionally and spiritually because I was prepared to manage the next level of success.

Then, one day, that voice inside me said, *now it's real*. Now that it was a part of me, it was a part of my personality (my DNA), it was who I had become. I had changed. Through this experience, I was transformed and changed to know how to show love despite how someone treats me. You can't directly control or be held accountable for how someone treats you, but you control how you treat others, and that's what it means to love everybody. This experience was less about someone not liking me. It was more about me growing and developing into the person I needed to become to fulfill what I had accepted as God's calling in my life.

Some people are placed in our lives that bring us adversity. Their relationship may be detrimental to our success and progress. It's important that we know and understand that when walking in faith, our steps are ordered by God. The people that bring us adversity are not our adversaries. God strategically places them in our lives to provide for us, stepping stones to the next level. They are brought on to change our direction to keep us on the path to success, not just success but good (sustainable) success. They are placed in our lives to help usher us into our destiny. So, we mustn't look at those who bring hardship or difficulty as our enemy. But instead, we should show them love and respect all the more because they are instrumental in making us great. That greatness is not determined by position, title, or money, but rather greatness is established by being able to treat others well despite how they treat you.

It's important to note that this was not a quick process. This did not take place over night. I dug deep inside and found that inward motivation. I trusted God's process for me. I didn't give up. I didn't quit. I sustained the kindness and consideration of this person for more than a year before I changed and began to realize the added blessings in my life. The important thing is that I continued until the change had come. Galatians 6:9 says, *let us not be weary in well doing: for in due season we shall reap if we faint not.* This simply means continuing to do good and don't get tired of doing what's right. Stay the course through difficult and uncomfortable situations and circumstances because your promotion, blessing, and success are waiting for you.

ABOUT THE AUTHOR

James Trent Williams was born in the small southwest Georgia town of Camilla, Georgia, in August 1965. Trent is the third of six children and the first of four boys. A graduate of Mitchell-Baker High School, Trent was very active and participated in several clubs and school activities. He was interested in sports, particularly basketball, where he played on the varsity basketball team. After high school, He attended Albany State University in Albany, Georgia, where he received a Bachelor of Science Degree in Management and a Master's in Business Administration.

Trent's first love was journalism. He was proficient as a writer. He was skilled enough as a writer that in his freshmen year at ASU, he won the top prize for being the student with the best journal entries in the fine arts department for the entire semester. However, he transferred to ASU's College of Business after his freshmen year, as his interest changed to banking.

He continued to expand his post-graduate education by completing a three-year Chief Executive Officer certification. The first year was at Warton, Executive Education, University of Pennsylvania. The second year was at Johnson Graduate School of Management, Cornell University, Ithaca, New York. The third and final year was at UVA Darden Executive Education, Charlottesville, Virginia.

Trent's employment experience includes a college internship with Penny Company as a merchandise manager, Ford Motor Credit as an Account Representative, and eleven years as a Vice President with Bank of America. With Bank of America, he worked in several capacities, which began with an 18-month comprehensive management training program, where he was trained in every banking area. In eleven years with Bank of America, he held Vice President of Retail, Commercial & Small Business Banking, and City Executive positions. Trent worked thirteen years with Heritage Bank of the South and Renasant Bank as Vice President, Commercial Banker, and

Compliance Corporate CRA Officer. For the last eight years, Trent has worked as Vice President of Lending Operations for DOCO Credit Union, and he's currently the Regional Vice President of Sales/Lending for Georgia's Own Credit Union's Southwest Region.

Trent is an ordained minister. He is married to Pamela Williams. Pam is an educator in the Dougherty School System. They have two adult children: a son, Jaylen, and a daughter, Camryn.

www.lifesinternaltherapy.com

Made in the USA
Columbia, SC
13 October 2024

44094866R00052